Light on The Fell

Langdale Ambleside Mountain Rescue Team: the first forty years

Edited by Phil Taylor

Light on The Fell

Langdale Ambleside Mountain Rescue Team: the first forty years

Published by

Langdale Ambleside Mountain Rescue Team

Lowfold

Old Lake Road

Ambleside

LA22 0DN

www.lamrt.org.uk

ISBN 978-0-9566433-0-8

Designed by Barry Marshall

Printed by Reeds Printers of Penrith

To all who have contributed over the years.

Contents

Acknowledgements

This team could not have evolved without the donations that we receive from the general public. Without these donations there would be no LAMRT. We wish to acknowledge the many people, too numerous to name individually, who have made a contribution, financial, practical or moral, to LAMRT over the past 40 years.

In the production of this book we would like to thank the following:

Nick Owen, Mark Bains and Roger Pickup proof read the text and helped with editing.

Paul Burke provided photographs of later years and converted old photographs into digital media.

Ashley Cooper provided photographs of later years.

Mo Richards, John Graham and Geoff Bowen supplied photographs and also information about the early years.

Olena Beal provided advice on design.

Contributors of written material are acknowledged in the text.

Efforts have been made to identify some early photographers without success.

Origins

Mark Bains

Mountain rescue of one form or another has existed in the Lake District for as long as travel or work has led people into the fells. Certainly it has a much longer history than mountaineering as a recreational activity. For an early illustration of how those who were able might respond to a fellside mishap, we need look no further than a 1783 account of the Hawkshead waller Frank Castlehow's retrieval of Wordsworth's schoolfellow John Benson, cragfast on 'Yewdale Crags' (probably Raven Crag, Tilberthwaite) after having been lured there in search of ravens' eggs and money from the farmers for their destruction[1].

On hearing of John Benson's plight he said that he and his son Jonathan would come along at once and see what they could do for the boy. After sending Will Tyson off, they made a bee line for the Yewdale Crag; and though he was on horseback they got there almost as soon as he did ... Frank roped his son Jonathan, and let him down on to the ledge not far from where John Benson was standing. In no time, or so it seemed, Jonathan had him back to where he could easily be hauled up ... The long wait on the crags till help arrived was terrible, Fleck said, and for John Benson it must have been a truly awful ordeal. ... Poor John was in a sad state when at last he was hauled up to safety; but thanks to Frank Castlehow, who tended and cared for him, he soon recovered sufficiently for the party to start on their descent of the crags, down which he was carried by the two wallers in turn. ... He never went crag climbing after ravens' eggs again; nor did Fleck.

We also have William and Dorothy Wordsworth to thank for what is the earliest detailed report of a mountain rescue in the Langdale area – and quite possibly anywhere. When news finally spread that George and Sarah Green had failed to return from a fair at Chapel Stile to their home at 'Blentern' (now Blind Tarn) Cottage,

Grasmere on 19 March 1808, it sparked a major search in wintry conditions that pulled together the entire community. Dorothy Wordsworth's emotive account, which was written to raise funds for the Greens' eight orphaned children, is heartbreaking; but anyone interested in mountain rescue cannot help but also be fascinated by the details. The incident began, as so many do now, with the momentous decision to stop waiting and take decisive action:

...at noon on Monday one of the Boys went to the nearest house to borrow a Cloak, and, on being asked for what purpose, he replied that his Sister was going to Langdale, as he expressed it, 'to lait their Folk' meaning to seek their Father and Mother, who had not come home again, as they had expected them, on Saturday. The Man of the house started up immediately, saying that 'they were lost!' – he spread the alarm through the neighbourhood, and many Men went out upon the hills to search, but in vain: no traces of them could be found ... On Tuesday as long as daylight lasted the search was continued. It was like a Sabbath in the Vale: for all the Men who were able to climb the heights had left their usual work, nor returned to it till the Bodies of the unfortunate Pair were found, which was on Wednesday afternoon. The Woman was first discovered upon some rough ground just above the mountain enclosures beside Mill Beck, in Langdale, which is the next stream or torrent to that which forms Dungeon Gill Waterfall ... Her Husband was found at no great distance: he had fallen down a Precipice; and must have perished instantly, for his Skull was much fractured[2].

Of course, not every Lakeland community had Grasmere's colony of poets and writers to chronicle its events and draw national attention to its local tragedies, and it is entirely possible that for this one well-documented incident, there have been many similar ones during the centuries that have gone unrecorded. And perhaps personal memories too motivated the Wordsworths to describe the incident so fully: they were themselves orphaned when their father died in 1783 as a direct result of spending an exposed winter night, lost and without shelter, on Cold Fell above Calder Bridge – again, perhaps a rare recorded example of a not so uncommon occurrence? But however usual or unusual, the Greens' sad tale, like that of the hapless Hawkshead schoolboy, has all the basic features of a mountain rescue as we now know it: the alarm is raised, the word is spread, a plan made, and a team of willing and able volunteers hastily dispatched.

By the 1930s, the involvement of St John Ambulance volunteers had introduced a degree of formal organisation, but otherwise this makeshift pattern of response was still little changed, especially in the more remote areas. Rescues in Langdale – such as that of a young girl with leg injuries recovered from Jack's Rake in 1932 – were carried out with minimal equipment by farmers, shepherds, mountaineers and anyone else who happened to be in the area at the time:

I was affiliated to St John's. And we were called out one Sunday night ... just as it was beginning to go dusk, and we went up to Dungeon Ghyll, and the accident was on Pavey Ark. By the time we got half way up the mountain, it was snowing ... it was pretty desperate really, it was really a filthy night. We got up to the place where this girl was lying in the crag ... and they decided that it would be easier to get down to her from the top rather than climb up to her because of the conditions, and yours truly being a small fellow, and light, they lowered me down on a rope. ... And there was quite a number of us – a few mountaineers that were there at the time were giving a hand. ... And the farmers helped us down and we had old hurricane lamps that the farmers had for their barns ... they were holding us by the ankle and helping us down ... and at the New Dungeon Ghyll before they altered the bar [when] it was a little wooden hut they put her onto the bar counter and old Dr Quarmby was going to take the boot off and attend to her on there but couldn't get a knife sharp enough to cut her boot off.[3]

These ad-hoc bands of helpers were the immediate forebears to the organised and dedicated mountain rescue teams that began to form in the Lake District from the 1940s onwards. Local knowledge began to be supplemented by formal training, and the first purpose-built stretchers started to replace the more traditional five-bar gate. As rock climbing grew in popularity, so mountain rescue developed as an institution, and in the valleys of Lakeland the two activities shared the same early pioneers. In Langdale it was Sid Cross MBE (1913-98), landlord of the Old Dungeon Ghyll Hotel from 1949, who would call upon fellow climbers to help respond to news of an accident on the fells. During the 1950s a network of local climbers started to organise itself into an unofficial team – linked by telephone, supported by the local police and doctors, and centred around Sid and the ODG. However, these developments still predate an official mountain rescue service: the first milestone in LAMRT's own story was reached in 1965 when Sid formed the Langdale Mountain Rescue Team.

The second milestone came four years later. To alleviate the growing demands upon the new Langdale Team from the increasing number of people who were finding new ways of getting into scrapes in the fells, Stewart Hulse and Peter Bell established the separate Ambleside Fell Rescue Team in 1969. Again, the St John Ambulance brigade was integral to the team's origins, providing training opportunities for young ambulance cadets being an important part of its operation.

Less than a year later, in January 1970, Sid Cross retired to Clappersgate and the Old Dungeon Ghyll, under its new management, ceased to be a mountain rescue headquarters. By this time the two teams were already in close collaboration, and perhaps inevitably and after an initial training period, the two teams merged.

(Endnotes)

[1] See T W Thompson, Wordsworth's Hawkshead (ed. R. Woof), Oxford University Press, London, 1970), pp211-15

[2] Dorothy Wordsworth, 'A Narrative Concerning George & Sarah Green', republished in Remembering the Greens of Grasmere, the Wordsworth Trust, Grasmere, 2008

[3] Taken from the archives of the Ambleside Oral History Society

1970

31 callouts

Beginnings

"We had hardly any equipment; a stretcher, a few ropes and a first aid sack containing a few splints and bandages. It was all kept in the Land Rover at Wateredge. We were later offered space in the barn at Lowfold which we only rented at first. We still retained the cabin behind Old Dungeon Ghyll as an advance base."

Geoff Bowen

"We had little equipment; a thin rope tied round your waist several times was your 'harness', abseiling really was a pain and first aid was very basic (compared with today). Waterproofs were OK in dry weather. The Land Rover that came with the Langdale MRT became my responsibility and every Saturday it was given a routine maintenance check and a run up the Struggle. Communications were a big problem; once on the hill no contact was possible - not like today with good radio comms. It was a different world."

John Graham

The first call-out

"1 February 12.30 pm. A dental nurse eighteen years, slipped some twenty feet on Scout Crag, Great Langdale. Sustained back injuries. Adequately clad and shod. Brought down by team and conveyed by ambulance to Kendal Hospital."

Incident Officer's Report

"Although I started going out on rescues with the Team in 1970, females were not accepted so I didn't officially become a team member until 1973! It was then another 15 years before we got another female team member Those first years were perhaps the most challenging. No helicopters, very few radios - if you went out on a search you completed your 'bit', whatever happened, because there was no reliable recall! No personal team gear, no pagers or mobile phones - how different to today!"

Mo Richards

1971

27 callouts

"Beritex and British Oxygen Companies have helped the Team in their efforts to overcome radio communication difficulties by contributing a Sounding Balloon and Helium Gas to lift a specially designed aerial to heights up to two hundred feet."

Equipment Officer's Report

The first sheep gathering incident

"26 July 3.00 pm. Shouts for help heard in the area of Stake Pass. Team alerted after confirmation from other people at the Dungeon Ghyll Old Hotel. On arrival at foot of Stake Pass shouts proved to be shepherds gathering sheep. False alarm with good intent."

Dick Barron Incidents Report

Forty years later this type of incident still occurs regularly.

"We purchased a second Land Rover – a long wheelbase station wagon seating twelve people ... enabling some members of the Team to follow on in a call-out. A new exhaust was fitted after protests of excessive noise from both engine and occupants. The Number 1 Land Rover is in good condition, perhaps a little scrape here and there with the rear offside corner having been replaced three times, and a new half shaft was called for on one occasion. Possibly one journey up Mickleden too many!"

John Graham Annual Report

1972

28 callouts

The first Bell Stretcher

Team member Peter Bell was given the job of developing a new split stretcher funded by a £100 donation from Mrs I Woods. Bell Stretchers subsequently became the most commonly used mountain rescue stretchers in England and Wales and are still used by the majority of teams today.

Lowfold Barn was bought

Due to the generosity of Miss Bell the team was able to buy the barn, which had previously been rented. Team members began extensive internal alterations.

Mine rescue followed by lightning strike

"On 22 July the Team was asked to assist Coniston MRT when an American boy fell 200ft down a Coniston mine shaft. He was finally brought to the surface at 4.00 am after a ten-hour operation. He sustained serious multiple injuries, but survived. On the following day whilst en route to a walker reportedly in difficulty on Bowfell, we were diverted to rescue a couple who were struck by lightning in Mickleden. They both survived despite nine ewes and eight lambs being killed only a few yards away by the same strike."

Mo Richards

"After a committee discussion it was agreed that females should not be admitted onto the call-out list, or the list of team members, but if any wife wishes to accompany her mate on a practice or rescue, they will be made most welcome."

Team Newsletter 1 May

1973...

30 callouts

Entonox was used for the first time

Entonox, an analgesic consisting of oxygen and nitrous oxide gas, was acquired to reduce severe pain in injured casualties. Today it is used routinely by mountain rescue teams across the UK.

Alterations to Lowfold were completed

"The Lowfold Base ... has been completely remodelled inside and now provides good storage for our two Land Rovers and other equipment, together with a drying room, lecture room and control desk. This must be the finest of its kind in the country".

Geoff Bowen Chairman's Report

Flares and lights

"17 August Small party of team searched Wansfell after a report was received by police that flares and torch lights had been seen. Search negative."

W Barron Incidents Report

(Flares and lights are still reported on the fell every year. Sightings of lights sometimes turn into genuine rescues, but in forty years we have not had a single rescue instigated solely by a flare.)

D of E groups

"22 September Male 17 years, on a D of E Award scheme. He suffered from exposure and was brought down from The Band by the team and conveyed to hospital

22 September Male 16 years, on a D of E Award scheme when he suffered exposure in Crinkle Ghyll. He was brought down the fell by the team and taken to hospital."

W Barron Incidents Report

(Incidents involving D of E groups seem to have been much more common in the seventies and eighties than they are today)

New Land Rovers

Two new Land Rovers were bought at a total cost of £3,600.
They were paid for by a grant of £2,000 from Westmorland County Council, £900 team funds and the sale of the two old vehicles. One of the Land Rovers was equipped with a Pye Westminster radio. The Team also had five Bantam radios to carry on the fell.

...1973

30 callouts

Our first search dog

In January Malcolm Grindrod graded his Irish Setter Jan to become our first SARDA dog handler.

Telephone call-out system

"All the local police stations have a list of ten team members – among which are six group call-out leaders who call out three or four other team members ... ... A further improvement – in the form of a lifeboat-type maroon call in Ambleside to back up the phone system – could perhaps be useful."

David Earnshaw Annual Report

Land Rover on rails

"The two Land Rovers parked side by side have only a few inches to spare fore and aft ... there is only one door which is wide enough for one vehicle only ... There are two steel rails set into the concrete floor and upon these run a set of four interlocked steel platforms, the position of each platform corresponding with the appropriate road wheel. Each of these platforms is fully supported on the rails by two strong wheels – thus forming a bogie. By this means it is a simple matter to push the Number Two Land Rover sideways along the garage floor. In the event of a mountain accident Number One Land Rover parked behind the main doors departs and then the second vehicle is pushed sideways so that it can be driven out."

Peter Bell Annual Report

"The Team was called after Ambleside residents heard shouts on Loughrigg. The first group drove up in a Land Rover to investigate and found the local refuse disposal lorry up to its axles in mud. The shouting had been the crew shouting instructions to the driver."

Team Newsletter

1974

33 callouts

The first helicopter rescue

On 24 June a 24-year-old climber fell eighty feet from Gimmer Crag sustaining serious head and other injuries. He was treated and carried about three hundred yards to a helicopter from RAF Acklington which was already in the area for a training exercise. The casualty was flown to Lancaster Royal Infirmary in seventeen minutes. This was the first time that a mountain rescue team and helicopter crew had worked together on a rescue.

Our first television appearance was on Pebble Mill at One.

Airbed racing rescue

A man was lucky to survive when he was found clinging onto a rock island in the river at Chapel Stile. He had been swept over a raging weir on the flooded river whilst 'airbed racing' after several days of torrential rain.

The first helicopter training

RAF helicopters did not work with civilian mountain rescue teams until Tony Richards and Stewart Hulse visited RAF Acklington to arrange a joint exercise for RAF and Lake District teams. This was held on 5 May and was attended by an RAF helicopter, LAMRT, Patterdale, Kendal and Coniston MRTs. An agreement was formed about how and when Lake District MRTs could call for helicopter assistance.

"At Langdale the 'chalet' behind the Old Dungeon Ghyll Hotel has been replaced by a new building provided by the Rotary Clubs of Windermere and Ambleside. A stretcher box with external access houses the equipment of the Mountain Rescue Post."

Geoff Bowen Chairman's Report

1975

37 callouts

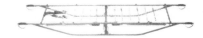

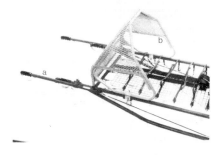

The Bell Stretcher: a. Extension handles, b. headguard.
(Lakeland Photographic)

Bell Stretchers

"Bell Stretchers are now in service with the RAF, the Police and with civilian rescue teams in the UK; elsewhere as far afield as the Andes, Jamaica and South Africa."

Peter Bell Annual Report

The Reviva, a portable warm moist air breathing device for the treatment of hypothermia, was used for the first time. This was also developed by Peter Bell.

Blackpool Tower abseil

"We did a Blackpool Tower Climb and Rescue Demonstration in aid of the British Limbless Ex-Servicemens' Association. Eric 'Spider' Penman abseiled from the top whilst half a dozen of us lowered a stretcher from halfway up the Tower."

Mo Richards

1976

39 callouts

The first landline connected radio

"During the summer we installed a Pye F27 base set at a position high above Ambleside on the lower slopes of Wansfell at Kelsick Annexe (part of Charlotte Mason College). This is linked by telephone line to Lowfold Base, where the control unit is housed. Thus Lowfold can be used to contact a wide area of fells hitherto out of range of the base."

Eric Penman Annual Report

Pavey Ark

"A 27 year old man from Preston left the Jack's Rake path on Pavey Ark by mistake and found himself going up a loose stone gully; he pulled a large stone on himself and fractured his right leg/ankle. The Team roped the stretcher and it was taken to the top of Pavey Ark. He was carried down the fell and then to hospital by ambulance to Kendal."

Stewart Hulse Incidents Report

(This casualty seems to have been luckier than most. Similar incidents still happen on Pavey Ark where injuries tend to be more serious.)

Whirlwinds and free beer

"I can clearly recall some very exciting helicopter flights in piston-engined Whirlwinds - in those days they liked to see how close to the corner of the rugby club they could get the rotors. The answer was very close indeed. I also remember our first issue of team kit - a heavy oiled wool jumper, and later a Henri Lloyd cag and a new fangled thing called a fleece jacket. And free beer in the ODG after every rescue. And the local bobby who was a team member at the time making sure I didn't miss out just because I wasn't then 18. Many of the older hands went out of their way to make a keen young lad welcome, but I do seem to remember doing a lot of fetching and carrying, and spending a lot of time as a body for the search dogs."

Mark Graham

1977

40 callouts

A new call-out system

"The GPO engineering section at Lancaster produced a circuit to operate 22 house bells in the Ambleside area. The circuit was so designed that it could be triggered by remote control ... Not all team members are within the scope of the bell circuit because some live beyond the Ambleside area. A few of these people can be reached by radio as soon as someone arrives at the base. The remainder are called, as before, by telephone."

Peter Bell Annual Report

Training progressed from ice axe braking on snow to front pointing on frozen cascades and the placement of ice screws. This gave confidence for the more difficult gully rescues and an insight into snow structure and avalanche protection.

This attention to winter competence and equipment results simply from the fact that whilst in summer it is possible to move about the fells without too much trouble, in the winter months even the easiest mountain path can become lethal – covered in ice or frozen snow-scree gullies become heavily corniced, and a slip can send the unwary many hundreds of feet at high velocity."

Training Report

Studded tyres

Metal studded winter tyres were fitted to team Land Rovers for the first time.

1978

43 callouts

"There will be few of us who will forget 11 February 1978 – a wintry Saturday when the team was stretched beyond limits with callouts coming in over a period of four hours – it was ten hours before everyone was back off the hill. Other teams were called in – Kendal, Patterdale and Keswick. An RAF team on exercise in the area also came to help; also an RAF helicopter, the Police, the Ambulance Service, the WRVS – all in appalling weather conditions, not only on the hill, but also on the roads."

David Earnshaw Secretary's Report

A rare picture – no less than three general practitioners who are members of a mountain rescue team in the Lake District about to take to the mountains in this exercise for "BMA News Review". They are (left to right) Dr David Earnshaw, Dr Ian Birket and Dr Geoffrey Bowen. One of them attends every emergency call-out to injured or lost climbers, or to tend to road accident victims.

"After the Rescue ...

If I may stand back and look at our Rescue Team, I see many skilled in mountain craft, some highly skilled in medical practice, many capable in the many aspects of rescue procedure, all prepared for prolonged endeavour under harsh conditions. But rescue does not end with the contacting, treatment and evacuation of the casualty.

In the case of fatalities, or injuries which prove fatal, there are the families or close friends to consider. They may be there on the fell beside you, or waiting down in the valley, or hundreds of miles away. In the latter case there may be little that the Team can do and I should like to commend the Police for the manner in which they attend to the necessary routine procedures. But even in such cases, the families may wish to visit the area, even have the funeral up here (as they are entitled to do), and here the Team are involved.

Bereavement at any time is a severe experience, but when far from home, perhaps on a fell top in extreme weather conditions, the shock and sense of loss can be greatly accentuated, and the greatest care and understanding is needed. Even after what must be a nightmare descent to the valley, the bereaved people have to face the necessary Police procedures, always sympathetically performed, and the prospect of spending the night in a busy hotel, a holiday cottage, or even a tent, which may be near unbearable. Here we are fortunate in that there are local families who are prepared to provide a bed and understanding; and may I mention that we are always pleased to receive names of any prepared, if necessary, to offer such true hospitality. On these occasions I am usually accorded the privilege of the responsibility as, in this field if no other, I have more experience than my fellow team members. I hope that I shall not be misunderstood when I say that, despite their sadness, the memories of many such encounters are very dear to me, and the links formed are deeply valued.

I would just add that during the average rescue there is a good deal of lighthearted banter and the casualty is likely to come in for a great deal of leg pulling, even to the extent of being told not to bother because, "if the worst comes to the worst the parson's here". But in the case of a fatality the proceedings are marked with reverence and there is always a brief moment when everything stops and together we commit the life to God."

Rev Graham Hartley Annual Report

1979

40 callouts

Snow and ice

"During the first three months of this year, for long periods the snow and ice isolated local residents from medical attention and food supplies were running low. Fell sheep had very little food because of the snow and many died of starvation. Number 2 Land Rover, fitted with snow and ice tyres, was pressed into service. Nearly every day this vehicle conveyed patients to the doctors' surgery and sometimes to hospital. We ... carried many tons of farm feed blocks to the stranded animals; the mode of transport being our mountain rescue stretchers which were sledged up the snow-covered valleys."

Stewart Hulse Annual Report

Sea king used for the first time

The new Sea king helicopter was used by the team for the first time on 29 January. Team members and avalanche probes were flown to Great End to search for three men thought to have been swept away by an avalanche. They were found the following day in Eskdale.

The caravan

"Andy Flitters acquired the caravan cheaply and converted it into a travelling canteen for fundraising events such as the Ambleside Festival and Galas. In fact it served as a multi-use 'vehicle', providing a mobile feeding station for long rescues and searches. I have known it on the odd occasion to be used as a temporary refuge for members who have been thrown out of their home after a slight domestic. I shall keep the former members' names secret as some are still living locally."

Mo Richards

1980

47 callouts

An ambulance was bought

A third vehicle was needed to supplement the two Land Rovers. A Bedford ambulance was bought at a cost of £9,086.

A record year

"1980 has proved to be the busiest year in the history of the Langdale Ambleside Mountain Rescue Team with 47 rescues ... Some team members are beginning to find it a strain as to how much time they can spend away from their families or from their places of work."

Eric Penman Team Leader's Report

1981

43 callouts

Improvements at Lowfold

"There has been a lot of activity at Lowfold Base this year and a lot of hard work put in by team members. We now have new sliding doors at the base, enabling all three vehicles to be garaged in the same part of the building. The other downstairs part of the base has been vastly altered by putting in extra walls. We now have another separate room which can be used for various purposes. The job of insulating the upstairs part of the building is in hand at the moment, so hopefully it should be a lot warmer in the near future."

Andy Flitter Chairman's Report

24 October

"38 Fellwalking The Band, Great Langdale 1.00 pm. A 46-year-old man from Whitley Bay suffered a fatal heart attack whilst out walking ...

39 Fellwalking Dow Bank, Silver How, Chapel Stile 2.15 pm. A 35-year-old female from Distington collapsed with a suspected heart attack ...

40 Karrimor Mountain Marathon Hanging Knotts Gully, Great Langdale 3.15 pm. Whilst trying to take a short cut on a fell race a 24-year-old female from Gwynedd fell in the gully and suffered spinal, head and rib injuries ...

41 Fellwalking The Band, Great Langdale 4.05 pm. ... went to the aid of a 13-year-old boy from Cheshire whose smooth-soled boots caused him to slip on a very wet fellside and suffer leg injuries ..."

Stewart Hulse and Brian Morgan Incidents Report

(This is not unusual. We still have quiet periods followed by several serious incidents on the same day.)

1982

49 callouts

The first team pagers

"In April the new pager system came into operation. This means that each individual in the Team carries a small pager all the time and in the event of a call-out, the simple dialling of a coded number by the Police will summon him and the other members of the Team at the same time. This has improved the attendance at callouts dramatically."

Andy Flitter Annual Report

Radios and pigeons

"Our radio gear now comprises 2 main base stations, one in Langdale and one in Ambleside; 2 mobile sets for use on the fell tops as relays; and 9 hand portable units. When the Team has to pay around £500 for just one hand portable unit, one might think it would be virtually indestructible. However, when one is pounding up the fell in torrential rain with a force-9 wind blowing, the poor set can manage only about two hours before it starts issuing noises similar to Donald Duck ... for all my many visits to Lowfold in the dead of night, soldering iron, screwdriver and prayer book in hand, there will still come the cry from the rest of the Team, 'We'd be better off with pigeons!'"

Tony Richards Radio Officer's Report

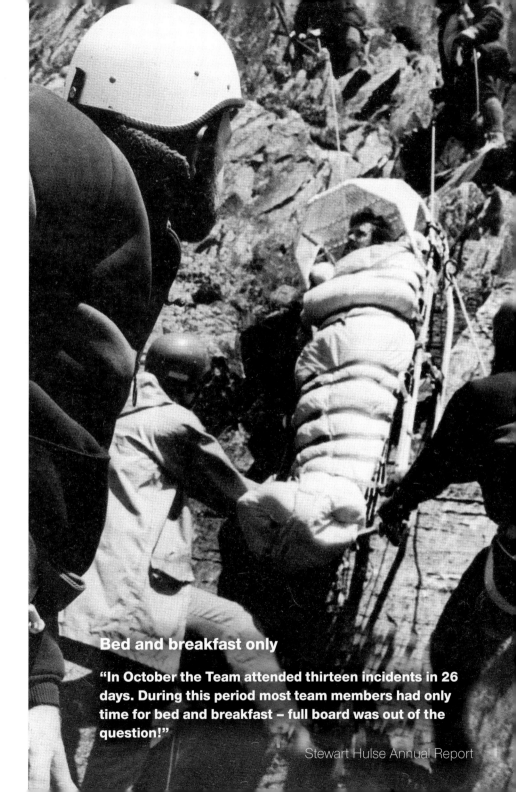

Rocket launcher

"We decided to improve our ability to deal with incidents involving people swimming or ice skating on mountain tarns. Life jackets, a one-man dinghy and a helicopter-type strop were bought.

We also obtained a Pains-Wessex rocket launcher which could fire a line six hundred feet. We got permission from the Police to test fire it over Wansfell. The test firing produced a lot of flames, noise and smoke. When the smoke cleared we could see the rocket stuck in a nearby tree. We abandoned the rocket idea, thinking that casualties might be in greater danger from our rocket than from drowning. We've since replaced rockets with throwlines."

Brian Morgan

Bed and breakfast only

"In October the Team attended thirteen incidents in 26 days. During this period most team members had only time for bed and breakfast – full board was out of the question!"

Stewart Hulse Annual Report

1983

52 callouts

There were eleven searches for walkers who failed to rendezvous with friends or relatives due to underestimating the time needed to complete their walk and became benighted without a torch or sufficient spare food and clothing.

"Most of our members would prefer to forget the long hot month of August, as during this period the Team answered no less than thirteen emergency calls."

Stewart Hulse Incidents Report

"My first reaction upon reading the 1983 Langdale Ambleside Mountain Rescue Team Report was, 'I'm glad I don't live in the Lakes!' It's not because of the lack of whiskey or midges, but the sheer volume of callouts ... once a week between the stretcher shafts is enough for any sinner."

Hamish MacInnes, Glencoe Mountain Rescue Team

1984

54 callouts

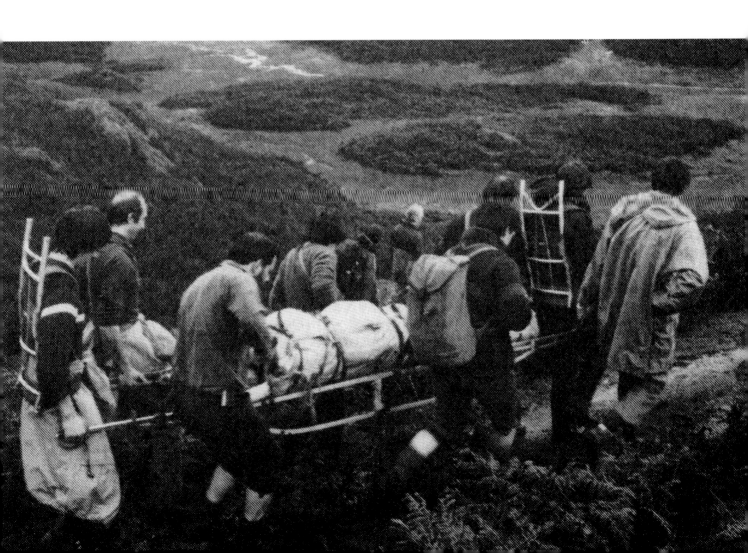

Troublesome Land Rovers

"One major worry this year concerns our Land Rover Ambulances. Both are ancient and have seen better days. This fact was brought forcibly home to us one day in summer when, on the way to an incident, the wiring of one Land Rover went up in flames. The resulting radio chatter was comical indeed! But the fire was extinguished and the journey completed. We have now mounted a special appeal for money to replace both vehicles."

Mo Richards
Equipment Report

Radio relays

"When I first joined the team any rescue in the high fells involved someone with a large rucksack containing a radio the size of a stereo and a car battery heading up to the highest vantage point in the area so that the radios the size of a brick, and just as heavy, could transmit back to base. The radio relay was usually consigned to the newest team member, as they were the most eager to please; the old hands had got past this level of eagerness. They sensibly stood back knowing that you would spend hours on top of a hill in the wind and the rain. With only the occasional radio message from the hill parties to pass back to base it could be a long and lonely wait in a small bivi shelter or crouched behind a boulder. Then there was the long stiff return to base as you tried to warm up the frozen body. How different to today's portable radios, permanent radio relays in every valley and GPS so base can track your every move."

Dave Till

1985

63 callouts

"**The extendable Clarke radio mast really came into its own this year when we used it to great effect as a relay aerial during two extensive searches in the Coniston area**"

Mo Richards Equipment Officer's Report

"I joined LAMRT at the age of 21, following in the footsteps of my father. I was born and brought up in Coniston; the mountains had always been quite a normal part of my life and being among the hills was second nature to me. I couldn't understand why the committee refused to have me at first because I was a woman. The committee view however was not the opinion of the main Team and I became a full member after the usual year's training, only the second woman to join after Mo. How the Team has moved on since those days!"

Joy Grindrod

New Land Rovers

"The main purchases of the year were two new Land Rovers to replace our 13-year-old models which were falling apart…The new Land Rovers are superb, safer, faster, more comfortable, more stable and more reliable than the old ones ever were. We now arrive at the head of Mickleden, Troutbeck, Rydal etc feeling normal and ready to effect a rescue instead of feeling sick, bruised and disorientated as was often the case in the past."

Mo Richards Equipment Officer's Report

The first Mountain Rescue Medical Seminar

"The initial momentum came from Stewart Hulse … a great enthusiast in always providing the best in immediate care …

The symposium was held over two days at Charlotte Mason College and approximately 130 delegates attended from mountain rescue teams throughout the United Kingdom."

David Earnshaw Annual Report

1986

46 callouts

FM Radios

Tony Richards, Peter Bell and David Pearson began testing FM radios. The work continued for a further two years before the old AM radio system was replaced. For a while LAMRT was alone in using FM radio so two sets had to be carried when working with other teams. But FM was obviously superior and soon became standard for all UK mountain rescue teams.

1987

59 callouts

Our first defibrillator

There were an increasing number of callouts to casualties with cardiac problems so a portable defibrillator was bought. It was massive and extremely expensive compared with modern AEDs. The photograph shows it attached to a specially constructed frame on a Bell stretcher.

Organising training

"The way training is organised should be changed to meet present-day needs. Traditionally almost all training sessions have been run by the Training Officer. If several people were responsible for running the training sessions ... this would lead, hopefully, to an improved quality of training sessions."

Mike Withers
Training Officer's Report

1988...

57 callouts

Advanced Casualty Care Group

"Six team members attended a course on setting up and giving intravenous injections and drips, thus improving the chances of some of our more seriously injured casualties."

Carl Wright Training report

"We used to practice cannulating on the false arm, but didn't get a feel for what it was like to cannulate a real arm, so we started training on each other. That's when the fun started – there was blood everywhere."

Keith Morgan

Large casualty with leg injury

"Twenty two team members went to the assistance of a large gentleman reputed to be six feet four inches tall and weighing seventeen stones, who had slipped and fractured his right lower leg."

Stewart Hulse Incident Report

(Lower leg injuries still account for about half of all incidents and some casualties are still very heavy, but we prefer them to be very light.)

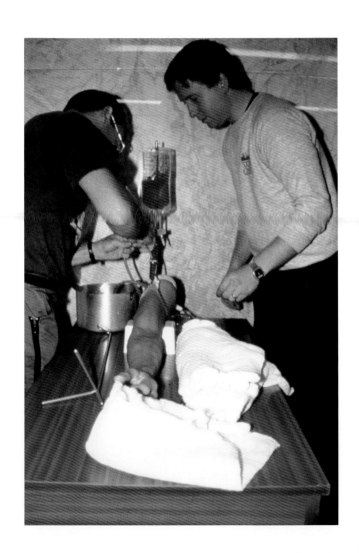

...1988

57 callouts

Lockerbie Disaster 21 December

"The most disturbing and awesome incident of 1988 was the Lockerbie disaster. Those of us who accompanied the SARDA dogs over a period of eight days will never forget the carnage and suffering which came to that little Border town."

Stewart Hulse

"The first thing I heard about the Lockerbie disaster was a phone call during the evening requesting the help of search dogs to assist with a plane crash on the M74. It was hard to take in what had happened, but the images that started to come through on the telly confirmed everything. That was when my father was a handler in the Team and I was a trainee handler with my first dog Anna. Dad went to help that evening and stayed for a few days. The night of the crash, the handlers found 120 bodies. For one handler it was her first callout ... another handler worked in the crater amongst all the aviation fuel. Not good! I went with the Team to assist with directing the search areas. I was 24. I will never forget seeing the rim of one of the jet engines which was embedded a foot below the surface of the pavement, the rest of it being buried to a great depth. I could not even begin to comprehend the force of the impact as it had hit the ground. It had landed only a few feet away from a row of council houses. A farmer spoke to my Dad, explaining to him how he was lucky to be alive. He showed him the other three jet engines that had landed in a circle close to his house. The images of the Lockerbie disaster are still etched into my memory to this day.

Joy Grindrod

"At the Lockerbie disaster SARDA found 120 of the crash victims during the first night. I worked at Lockerbie for eight days, only going home for Christmas Day. Two days after I got back from Lockerbie my dogs Spin and Mist made a brilliant find - a walker who had fallen off Neck Band Crag on the Band. Unfortunately the guy died of his massive injuries before we had evacuated him. How nice it would have been to save a life after Lockerbie."

Malcolm Grindrod

1989

61 callouts

"Anna, my first dog, was graded Novice Search Dog at two years old. Our assessment was held over four days in the North Lakes where we worked in a different location each day. I remember getting up each morning to a blizzard. During the third area on the third day the stress and constant blizzards finally got to me and I sat down in the middle of my search area and had a good 'boo hoo'. Then I felt so much better. I got up, carried on searching and quickly made a find. We passed the course and a year later Anna graded as Full Search Dog.

Anna was a lovely dog; she enjoyed working and loved everybody. She retired at the age of thirteen, and died just before she was seventeen."

Joy Grindrod

VW Synchro

The old Bedford ambulance was replaced by a new VW Synchro four-wheel-drive ambulance.

1990

73 callouts

"The collie seems to have evolved over the years to be the favourite among SARDA handlers. It is small, intelligent and easy to train. Size is an important factor for obvious reasons, but I can remember my collie fighting with Dave Riley's collie on a double winch into a helicopter fifty feet above the ground. Dave's entrance into the chopper was, shall we say, unusual – he was wearing his dog like a Davy Crockett hat."

Malcolm Grindrod. SARDA report

19 May, a busy day

"Search, Stickle Tarn 6.00 am

Two men bivvi'd out on Tarn Crag after a 'liquid supper'. The next morning one staggered down the hill with a head injury saying his friend had 'gone missing'. The Team with assistance from SARDA, RAF St Athan and RAF Boulmer found him with severe exposure. Moral: don't walk up the hill at night after drinking Old Peculiar!

Scrambling, Stickle Ghyll 12.57 pm

A 43-year-old man fell in the waterfalls and sustained head and leg injuries.

Para gliding, Wrynose Pass 4.15 pm

A 26-year-old woman tried to avoid another paraglider and crashed, fracturing her leg.

Fellwalking, Far Easedale 10.00pm

Two women were walking down Far Easedale. Woman A left Woman B to make her own way down because B was 'too slow' and made no arrangements to meet up again. A booked into a guest house and raised the alarm when B failed to turn up. A search with the help of SARDA failed to find B who was safe and well in another guest house!"

Andy Carling Incidents Report

1991

73 callouts

Insurance and uniforms

In his Team Leader's Report, Stewart discussed the concept of uniforms and identification of mountain rescue teams, as well as compulsory insurance. Nearly twenty years later both these subjects are still hotly debated. The insurance issue regularly rears its head, although it is rarely raised by someone from inside MR. More commonly it is by an outsider with little understanding of the history or philosophy of mountain rescue, or more significantly, how it might actually improve the service!

With mountain rescue teams regularly working on large scale disasters and incidents, being identifiable to other emergency services and members of the public is increasingly important. The nature of what we do means that an actual uniform isn't practical, but over time, red and black have become the colours of choice for most teams and vehicle livery is becoming more consistent. The addition of high-visibility vests makes it much easier to mix with other agencies in these circumstances.

Nick Owen

"The pager is going off – 2 fallen climbers in Dungeon Ghyll! My first real rescue – very different from first aid training in the base – there are real people scattered about with real injuries, which look life threatening to me! But the team moves into gear smoothly and calmly and small groups surround each casualty rendering first aid to stabilise the situation. Somebody talks calmly into the radio to ensure that the next phase of the evacuation comes together to deliver our fellow climbers to the definitive care they need at Furness General Hospital. I even help a little bit by assisting an experienced member of the Team in patching up our casualty. So this is Mountain Rescue!"

Dave Almond

1992

83 callouts

"Search, Rydal Valley, 25 September Two groups reported hearing 'positive' shouts for help. Nothing found. The farmer and local hunt had been in the valley. I believe one of the farmers has a sheepdog called Help. Nothing else could explain the frequency of this type of incident."

Andy Carling Incidents Report

Chocolate biscuit incident.

"One of our faster team members arrived at the scene of a collapsed walker who had all the symptoms of a serious heart attack ... By pure chance, a doctor appeared on the scene ... Viewing the casualty from a standing position, the doctor said, 'Give him a chocolate biscuit, that'll do the trick', and off he went down the fellside, leaving Dave to cope alone. A few minutes later, the Team arrived, gave the appropriate drugs and placed the casualty on a monitor. It was later confirmed ... that the casualty had suffered a major heart attack. Nobody seems to know to this day what therapeutic value there is in a chocolate biscuit."

Stewart Hulse Review of the Year

1993...

76 callouts

Ada's Nook

"The beginning of the year saw the completion of the refurbishment of the small building next to the base which used to be a wash house and outside loo. The building was in a very dilapidated state and if nothing had been done with it, it would have collapsed. Fortunately our good friend Ada came up trumps, and not only paid for the refurbishment of the building, but also the building of a storeroom within the base.

This means that we now have a small room which can be used for training sessions, committee meetings, etc. But it also serves a very special purpose during a search or rescue; we now have somewhere, away from the hustle and bustle in the base, where, if need be, friends and relatives can wait undisturbed.

Previously we have tended to concentrate on the needs of the person being rescued and may have not given enough thought to those that were with them. It has now become apparent how much those who have used 'Ada's Nook' appreciate somewhere quiet and comfortable to wait."

Andy Flitter Chairman's Report

"Coming across your first fatality is never easy, especially if it is a fallen climber as opposed to a heart attack victim. I don't suppose it really gets any easier over time - maybe you just learn to cope with it a bit better. Certainly being part of a supportive team helps. Fatalities are the downside of the job - if that sounds callous, it's probably a coping mechanism. Trying to keep emotionally detached is not always easy. The big upside of our role is the feeling of satisfaction, of a job well done, when a life has been saved. It more than compensates for the long hard carries, the cold wet night searches and the occasional ungrateful idiot."

Ashley Cooper

...1993

76 callouts

A portable fax machine

The practices of 'stay and play' or 'scoop and run' took a potential step forward when the Team acquired a portable fax machine, which when connected to a (quite large) mobile phone, could send printouts from our ECG monitor to hospital for analysis. Essentially a good idea, it failed to catch on, partly because mobile phone signals were even poorer then than now; the equipment was heavy, and when it came down to it, very few doctors had time to sit next to their fax machines waiting for us!

Radios for all team members

Thirty hand portable radios were purchased: enough to be allocated personally to each team member. Previously radios were kept at base, and update information to team members on the location or nature of an incident.

The first time you arrive at an incident first is a rite of passage for any mountain rescuer, it's also potentially terrifying! My first time was on 1 January 1993. Two young lads had been climbing a semi-frozen Dungeon Ghyll. The ice broke off and the leader fell 65 feet or so onto his second, followed by most of the ice and a quantity of rock. Both of them ended up in the freezing ghyll with multiple injuries and I got there first! Obviously the two lads needed immediate help, the other people who had gone to their aid were expecting something similar, and all I could think was 'Oh s**t! What a mess! What now?! PANIC...no...ABC... Airway, Breathing, Circulation. No! Personal safety first, then ABC. They're groaning, that's the A and B sorted (you can't groan if you can't breathe), what about the C?' Then someone else arrived, and then another and more. The pressure was off and I stood back and watched them go to work. I'm not sure I contributed anything useful to the rescue. They worked with a confidence that I doubted I would ever acquire. Well rehearsed sequences of checks and treatment were carried out. I don't think anyone noticed the fact that I was still shaking an hour later! Both survived and I didn't get scared off - I'm still involved 17 years later!"

Nick Owen

1994

110 callouts

"When I joined I looked in awe at the skills other team members had and sixteen years later I look at the current team members and still feel the same. Fitting in with a group of grumpy middle-aged mountain rescuers was a daunting task only successfully completed by becoming one!"

Roger Pickup

1995

82 callouts

Better pagers

Tone only pagers were replaced with vodapage message pagers, a vast improvement in communicating callout information, allowing rendezvous points, injuries and other useful information to be passed.

Advanced casualty care

"Once a month a small, furtive group gather secretively with tourniquets, hot drinks and an eye for a vein; far from being involved in illegal practices, we are training in antravenous cannulation so that appropriately skilled team members can set up a means of giving intravenous fluids to the seriously injured casualty ... By regular practice on each other and adherence to a strict protocol, we are pleased to be pushing forward in terms of mountain rescue care."

Paul Davies Medical Report

"A boy mountain biking Coast to Coast with his father and sister fell off and injured his ankle. His sister didn't believe him and said so. However, without the benefit of an x-ray machine and the intuition that an older sister has, we had to take his word for it. He even managed to whimper and yelp as we carried him down. However, her diagnosis of 'LYING LITTLE RAT' was correct."

Nick Owen Incident Report

GPS tests

Although GPS navigation was treated with some suspicion, the Team began experiments to see if it might be useful on searches in darkness and bad weather. The two units used were donated by Field and Trek. It would still be a while before they were in general use.

1996

80 callouts

The story about a couple using their mobile phone to request a helicopter to rescue them because they were late for their dinner appointment first appeared in our annual report in 1996. The story was attributed to an unknown mountain rescue team and appears to be untrue; an urban myth!

Our first encounter with a personal locator beacon

26 October at 18.50

"A party of three in their thirties phoned from 'Three Tarns' to say they were lost in the mist and dark, and to ask if we could guide them off. This is always difficult to do since if their exact location is not known then we can't know for sure where we're sending them, and their having no torch didn't help. We sent a party up to locate them. On the phone one of them revealed that he had a 'personal locator beacon', a device for locating crashed aircrews at sea. We discussed the matter with the RAF and they said they could pin-point it if a helicopter could fly low over it a couple of times. This worked, and the three were picked up and flown back to Ambleside. Their actual location was on the other side of Crinkle Crags, two miles from where they thought they were! Their equipment was non-existent. They had no waterproofs, food, lights or map, but had managed to pack the mobile phone and personal locator beacon. Not what we'd call 'getting your priorities right.' If the weather had closed in and the helicopter had not been able to fly over, all three probably would have died before we had found them. Modern technology is all well and good, but in the hands of an idiot, could potentially be lethal. None of these pieces of equipment keep you warm, give you energy, or show the way home; only common sense and planning will do this."

Nick Owen Incident report

The Bread Van

After several clutch replacements, our VW Synchro ambulance was replaced with a much tougher wide bodied Land Rover 110. It was commonly referred to as 'The Bread Van', but was sometimes given less complimentary names from team members travelling in the back.

1997

91 callouts

Ice rescue sledge

We bought an ice rescue sledge which had to be imported from the USA because nothing like it was available in the UK at the time. It can be inflated within a few seconds using pressurised CO_2 and allows a rescuer to slide towards a casualty who has fallen through thin ice. Ropes are used to pull the sledge, rescuer and casualty back to the shore.

New GPS units were bought

Eight Eagle Explorer GPS units were bought for use on night searches. They were more user friendly than previous GPS devices and marked the beginning of the general acceptance of this type of equipment.

Rob's GPS tracking project

Rob Brookes spent a long time developing a GPS tracking system which could display team members' positions on an electronic map. He managed to make it work, but the prototype was too big to be routinely carried on the fell. The equipment shown here would need to be taken in addition to the usual radio used for voice, and the GPS unit needed to be held in the hand where it could see the sky. Additionally, a large lead acid battery was needed to give enough power to work for about three hours. But it did prove that the concept would be viable as soon as smaller components were available. Development would continue for a further nine years before becoming the MRMap that we use today.

1998

77 callouts

First Team Website

Paddy was graded as a search dog

"Having a search dog and finding people hidden on hill sides during practices is very satisfying. Working with a dog that finds a group of casualties, some of whom might not have survived the night in sub zero temperatures and high winds, is a unique experience elevated with a sense of pride."

"Does that search dog work for you' I'm often asked. 'No' I reply 'we're a team and more often than not he makes me look good!' So what's my contribution to the search? I feed the dog"

Roger Pickup

Fallen climber

A 35-year-old man was seriously injured when he fell one hundred feet while climbing Raven Crag, Great Langdale. He was treated by team members and a Coniston GP who happened to be climbing nearby at the time of the accident.

Dislocated finger

"Fellwalking, Mill Ghyll, Great Langdale. The husband of a 38-year-old woman phoned 999 when she slipped and dislocated her finger a few hundred yards above the bridge near the bottom of the Ghyll. We were a little surprised at their apparent inability to deal with this one themselves."

Nick Owen Incidents Report

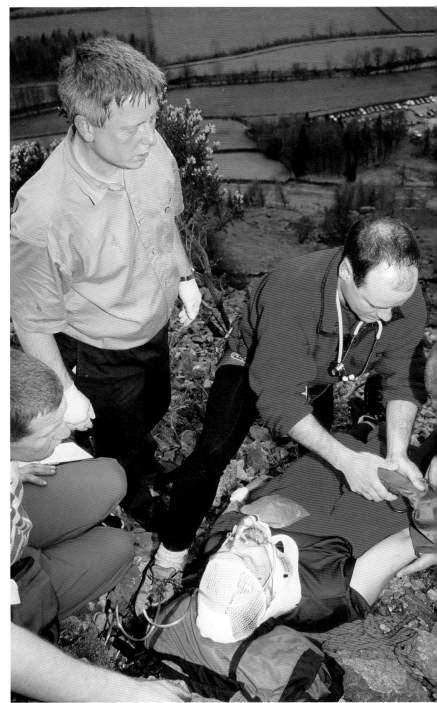

1999

72 callouts

"When I first joined the Team someone warned me that the most dangerous part of a rescue was rushing into the base at the start. It was too easy to bang your head on the top of the low entrance. Then you could fall down two uneven steps where the next person to trip would land on top of you. A good enough reason for a new base!"

Phil Taylor

Mountain Rescue Bomb Squad

"Search and recovery, Easdale Tarn, Grasmere. 4 April at 13.32

A visiting senior policeman spotted a cylinder-type object under a stone and reported a bomb to Cumbria Police. We were sent to investigate and the bomb disposal people were alerted. We found the suspect device to be a conventional smoke flare and carried it down."

Nick Owen Incidents Report

Fundraising started for a new base

The old building was three hundred years old. All previous development had been within the original building which was no longer efficient to maintain. There were too many nooks and crannies and one of the Land Rovers had to be kept outside because the garage was too small. But the location was suitable with good road access and there were no other suitable sites or buildings available in Ambleside. The old base would need to be demolished and a new one built on the same site.

2000

77 callouts

New year's eve

"On New Year's Eve we went out during the early afternoon on a 'small' search. I was gullible enough to tell my visitors I'd be back soon. A couple had become lost near Calf Crag in a blizzard. We struggled through chest deep drifts and kept being blown off our feet before we resorted to crawling. We found the casualties during the early evening and got home just before midnight. I remember flimsily clad partygoers looking very surprised as they fell out of pub doorways and watched me push my bike home through deep snow. My visitors made their own tea and I learned that 'small', when applied to a search, has nothing to do with the time or effort it'll take."

Phil Taylor

Old dog, new tricks?

"Having already spent thirty years in mountain rescue including fifteen as Team Leader of one of the Mid Pennine teams, I was chuffed to bits about getting through LAMRT training. It wasn't just about assessment of skills: it included how to blend in and make whatever contribution you can. And trying to emulate the total commitment of established team members whilst still having fun."

Dave Barrington

A limited company

"The new base has been designed and planning permission granted. We now need to raise up to £500,000 to fund the scheme. As this entails such a large sum of money, the committee took the decision to turn LAMRT into a Limited Company, whilst retaining our charitable status."

Roger Pickup Treasurer's Report

2001

51 callouts

The fells were closed due to Foot and Mouth Disease

"What a time to take over the leadership of the team! We didn't do a job for three and a half months due to the foot and mouth outbreak ... I was the butt of a number of jokes from the team members as the team leader who had never done a job. I countered this by telling the team that I'd given them the summer off. I don't think they believed me."

Nick Verrall Team Leader's Report

TETRA trial

We worked with DTI, Lancaster University and Simoco to trial TETRA (Terrestrial Trunked Radio) This included transmitting digital photographs and medical telemetry directly from a casualty site to base or hospital for the first time. The technology was very advanced and our TV appearances included BBC's Tomorrow's World.

"The fells had only been officially reopened for three hours, following relaxing of FMD regulations, when we were called out to assist a 51-year-old man who had collapsed with a suspected heart attack."

Nick Owen Incidents Report

Stewart Hulse received an MBE and the MRC Distinguished Service Award.

Base redevelopment

"We have obtained all planning consents and our architect has completed a full set of plans. We have purchased property adjacent to the base, without which we could not proceed, and we are in a position to start building as soon as we are sure we have sufficient funding."

Peter Ennis Annual Report

2002

52 callouts

Ambleside coach crash and a long fall

On 8 June a coach carrying more than forty passengers crashed through a garden wall and overturned near the bottom of Kirkstone Road. Police, ambulance service, air ambulance and fire service attended. We used our vehicles to transport the less seriously injured passengers. Lowfold was used as a clearing station where casualties were assessed before being taken to the most appropriate hospitals.

Whilst this incident was ongoing a woman fell approximately one hundred feet down Raven Crag, Great Langdale whilst trying to find a safe descent route for her family. She suffered multiple injuries to her head, neck and spine. We treated her on scene and she was airlifted to hospital by Royal Navy helicopter. Kendal MRT assisted.

Base redevelopment

The National Lottery Community Fund awarded us a grant and the old base was demolished in November to allow building to begin. Our temporary base was a terraced house on Lake Road opposite the telephone exchange. We completed the move in a single day and still had time for a search on the same evening! During the building work we kept two Land Rovers in an old metal container on the building site. The others were kept behind the telephone exchange and on Hayes car park.

Coach stuck in snow

"A coachload of people on a two day tour of the Lakes nearly spent both days on their coach when it got stuck in snow at Kirkstone Pass. We ferried fifty two of them down to Ambleside. 'Road Closed' signs were in place."

Nick Owen Incidents Report

2003

81 callouts

Relatives' Room

The new base includes a comfortable relatives' room where distressed relatives or close friends are cared for during protracted searches or during the hours following the death of a casualty. Money to furnish the 'Relatives Room' and some other parts of the building was provided by the Lady Ann Rooker Memorial Fund.

"Fellwalking somewhere, Cumbria

We received a call via the Police from a man who was - requesting help. He only seemed to know that he was in Cumbria. Questioning revealed that he was on Helvellyn. Further investigation revealed that his only problem was that he needed to contact his friend and had run out of credit on his phone. He had contacted the police because he didn't need credit to dial 999! It was suggested that he sorted himself out. I understand a different expression was used, but I can't use it here."

Nick Owen Incidents Report

New base completed and paid for

Building work continued for most of the year and we finally moved into the new building in November, just a year after moving out of the old one.

"At the end of the year, we have been able to take a deep breath, balance the books and maintain our reserve funds which have fluctuated more than the Dow Jones Index over the year!"

Incident 78

"A young woman collapsed, reported as diabetic and pregnant. Her partner called us for help, but didn't know where they were... We eventually located them just as it was going dark. The woman was very cold and unable to move, the man cold, but still able to walk. The woman was treated for hypothermia and evacuated to the valley on a stretcher. The man was given additional clothing and escorted down. They had no map or compass, no torch, no spare clothing, no waterproofs and it is certain the woman would have died before daybreak had we not found them. Their clothing was totally inadequate for the fells in any conditions, let alone in the rain, hail and thunder and lightning that we encountered trying to find them."

2004

100 callouts

"The team was asked to assist in a major operation to find and rescue a large number of cockle pickers from the sands in Morecambe Bay. They had been caught by a fast advancing tide. A number of people made their own way to safety, several were rescued, but tragically nineteen drowned. The team sent vehicles, personnel, search dogs and specialist radio equipment. On 15 February another body was located on the sand near Morecambe … A twenty-first body was subsequently located in early summer."

Nick Owen Incidents Report

"My first rescue as a full team member was to a fallen climber on Gimmer Crag. It was Father's Day and the casualty had been climbing with his young son. I remember how relieved the young lad was when we arrived and when were able to ease his father's pain. I also remember his excitement (and mine) as the Sea King arrived and hovered close to the crag."

Keith Birch.

New high band radios brought GPS tracking closer

We needed to get new radios as radio frequencies were changed from low band to high band for all UK mountain rescue teams. Lakes teams chose Simoco radios largely because Simoco planned to release a speaker microphone containing a GPS chip, bringing a practical tracking system much closer.

Helicopter epic

On 17th May we were called to a scrambler who had fallen onto a ledge high on the Mickleden face of Pike O'Stickle. A Royal Navy helicopter and Kendal MRT were called to assist. The helicopter main rotor clipped the crag causing serious damage and forcing the helicopter to pull away suddenly, dragging a Kendal team member off the crag. The team member fell a considerable distance onto another ledge, suffering serious spinal injuries and a broken arm. The helicopter landed very heavily, but upright, near the bottom of Rossett Ghyll. The helicopter crew and another Kendal member still on board were shaken, but unhurt.

A second operation was organised to rescue the injured Kendal team member who was treated on the ledge before being airlifted to Carlisle. The original casualty was then recovered and flown to hospital.

The following day an RAF mountain rescue team member fell approximately one hundred feet, sustaining multiple injuries, while clearing debris from the crash site. He was treated at the scene and flown to hospital by helicopter.

A couple of days later we watched an army Chinook recover the damaged Sea King. Being mindful of possible embarrassment to the Royal Navy, we only transported a single television cameraman to the end of Mickleden.

2005

84 callouts

Large search

A man was missing from home and there was concern for his safety. We searched the Langdale area overnight and for the following three days, assisted by SARDA, Duddon and Furness, Kendal, Bowland Pennine and Coniston MRTs, Cumbria Ore Mines Rescue Unit and Police divers. He was eventually located in his tent on a local campsite. He had returned to the area after going elsewhere to avoid being found!

Vehicle rescue

"We were asked to rescue a woman stuck in a vehicle on Loughrigg Terrace. Assuming the vehicle to be a large 4X4, we turned up with a heavy towrope and thought we might use the Land Rover winch. We felt somewhat over-equipped when we arrived to discover an electric mobility scooter with a flat battery."

Lucy Noble

2006

100 callouts

Team member injured in Crinkle Ghyll

We went to the aid of a scrambler with a suspected ankle injury high up in Crinkle Ghyll. The location was difficult and weather conditions were atrocious with low cloud and very heavy rain causing the beck to rise in the Ghyll. Whilst approaching the scene a team member fell in the Ghyll and received a painful chest injury. A group of us went to his aid while the rest continued to the original casualty. After some spectacular flying in difficult conditions, an RAF Sea King managed to winch both casualties out of the Ghyll. The coldest and wettest rescue for a long time!

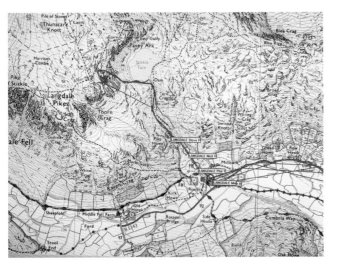

A working GPS tracking system at last!

Simoco gave Rob a pre-production GPS speaker microphone which he tested for a further 6 months using software he wrote himself. Dave Binks of Duddon and Furness MRT took over the software development, Ordnance Survey agreed to supply free 1:25000 maps to all mountain rescue teams and MRMap was born. This is probably the most useful mountain rescue development since the radio was invented.

Moon boots

A 45-year-old woman fell one hundred metres from high on Red Screes whilst trying to descend hard névé wearing moon boots. She suffered a fractured femur, head, chest and back injuries. She was treated by team members and airlifted to hospital by RAF helicopter.

2007...

105 callouts

Grayrigg train derailment and a search

Our jobs often come in pairs. A couple reported themselves lost near Helm Crag, but just as we were beginning the search, we were diverted to help other emergency services at Grayrigg where a train had derailed and rolled down an embankment. We stretchered seriously injured casualties to helicopters and helped search surrounding fields for any dazed passengers who may have wandered off. Meanwhile Coniston MRT helped with our search and found the lost couple on High Raise.

Swiftwater rescue training

We bought new swiftwater rescue equipment and a group of team members completed a course to qualify as Swiftwater Rescue Technicians. Most team members now choose to do the course.

"We have attended more than forty incidents where there was nothing wrong with the people involved other than that they went up a mountain that they were never realistically going to get back down again without some outside help."

Nick Owen
Team Leader's Report

...2007

105 callouts

Driving team vehicles

We established a new driving policy. Everyone who drives team vehicles will be trained by a police driving instructor. All response drivers must first pass the police response driving course.

Moonbow

"We were requested to assist Coniston MRT with the recovery of two cragfast climbers on Dow Crag. The weather was clagged in and they were having trouble locating them ... As the weather cleared we spotted a moonbow. This subsequently led to much Googling to explain the phenomenon. Better than sitting at home watching Big Brother and getting old."

Nick Owen Incidents Report

"When you get your pager, it comes with a warning about the adrenaline rush of the first rescue. Mine involved a casualty with two broken ankles. My adrenaline and I rushed to the New Dungeon Ghyll, to find the others standing around scratching their heads and looking confused. The casualty had just walked her two broken ankles off the fell and gone home. 'It's not usually like this you know', I was told gruffly, as I tried to show that I was as good as the rest of them at responding to an emergency by standing around scratching my head and looking confused."

Mark Bains

Dungeon Ghyll accident

A man was hit by rockfall whilst scrambling and his lower leg was very seriously injured. We treated him in the bottom of the ghyll whilst being bombarded by more rocks before he was winched from the scene and flown to hospital by helicopter.

The incident was later re-enacted for the television programme, Britain's Bravest (shown below).

2008...

103 callouts

"I remember a man who fell from Jack's Rake. I couldn't believe just how many injuries he had and how suddenly it had happened to a normal guy having a nice day out. I've done that same route dozens of times and whilst always aware of the drop it had never occurred to me what actually happens if you fall off! I still go there regularly, but that image haunts me and I always breathe a sigh of relief when I'm safely past the point where he fell."

Keith Birch

Two new Land Rovers – Frank and Mavis

Mrs Mavis Mellor offered to replace one of our 15-year-old first response vehicles and we replaced the other one from team funds. The two new Land Rover Defenders were heavily modified to our requirements by Lakeland Land Rover. One was named Frank E Mellor whilst the other was named Mavis Mellor.

Gimmer Crag rescue

A young woman's knee became jammed in a crack on A Route, Gimmer Crag. We lowered team members to the ledge, but it proved very difficult to remove her knee from the rock so the rescue became very prolonged. We called Clapham based Cave Rescue Organisation (CRO) to assist with specialist rock splitting tools. An RAF helicopter lifted CRO and their equipment to the top of the crag. A Patterdale team doctor was called to anaesthetise the woman, but CRO' managed to free the knee without this being necessary. A further complication was that during this rescue we were called to rescue another woman with a knee injury on Gibson Knott. Kendal MRT assisted with both rescues. Remarkably, the Gimmer Crag casualty appeared to be uninjured by her ordeal and was able to go climbing again the following day.

Beinn became a fully graded search dog.

...2008

103 callouts

"Memories of my first search are darkness, cold, wet and being tired. It reminds me that what we do is not glamorous; these are the true conditions in which we often find ourselves working, and true commitment is needed to repeatedly put ourselves knowingly into these conditions. But above all, and most importantly, I distinctly remember the serious failing of my waterproofs!"

Marie Lynchey

"My first rescue was to a fallen climber on Gimmer Crag. The callout came during training on Windermere. Watching team members trying to remove dry suits in double quick time was hilarious. Soon the team was called to a number of night searches on Crinkle Crags. Going up and down the back side of the Crinkles several times in one night really emphasised the level of fitness required. I wondered whether or not I'd make it.

Seeing my first fatality was a shock, but particularly moving was the care and respect paid to the body by the team. I cried when a prayer was said."

Steve Pendered

2009...

133 callouts

New drugs guide

Les Gordon wrote A Plain English Guide to Drugs for Use in Mountain Rescue; useful when we need to know whether drugs being taken by a casualty will interact with drugs we consider administering.

SimMan

We bought 'SimMan', a scarily realistic advanced patient simulator. He breathes, speaks and has a pulse. He can be programmed to have seriously dangerous illnesses and injuries. But even more scarily, he reacts to our treatment pretty much as a real person would.

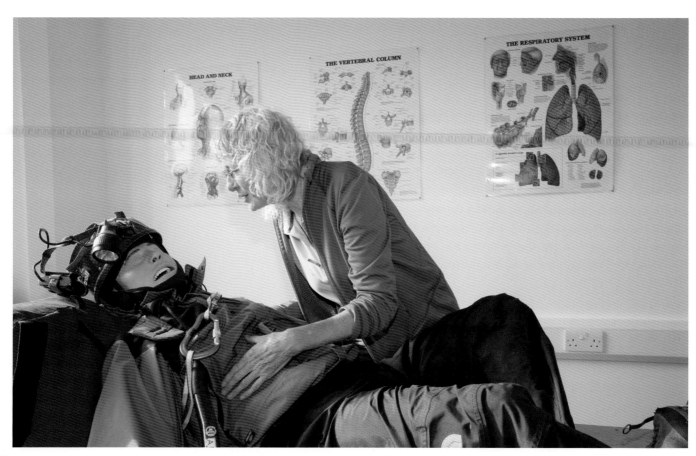

New training website

Our new training website stores easily accessible training information about everything from helicopters to how to use the dishwasher.

"My first rescue was a sheep stuck in a bog on Wansfell – not what I'd expected! After ten minutes of struggling we set it free and it ran off without even saying thank you!"

Graham Lobb

"The most frightening rescue was my first 'big' one. We set out before breakfast on empty stomachs, in sixty mile an hour winds and driving rain. The casualty had been blown off the path into Dungeon Ghyll. When a strong gust nearly blew me into the ghyll I seriously thought I was a goner."

Stephanie McDearmid

"The banter in the Team on the way down is a reason in itself to attend rescues!"

Steve Pendered

...2009...

133 callouts

More new Land Rovers

A new seven-seat people carrier and an ambulance completed our vehicle replacement programme. We now have four Land Rovers, identically equipped with full roll cages, extra driving lights and bonnet-mounted search lights.

"Our old Land Rovers were basic, simple, robust and generally got us to where we wanted to go off-road. Now we have Land Rovers that are comfortable, sophisticated, electronically enhanced and climb steep gradients controlled by a computerised engine management system. The single consistent problem over the years is the 'nut' who holds the wheel. We are currently training the 'nuts'".

Roger Pickup

Warning signs

We placed notices in Langdale warning people venturing onto the fells to be prepared for the winter conditions.

"I was still a trainee in February 2009, so when the pager went off, I was itching to get out. 'Search. Group of three stuck in Langdale.'

On the hill, the conditions were lethal for the ill-equipped. Despite seeing the team's warning signs regarding winter conditions, the hapless three continued their walk until becoming totally stuck. We found them in the Bright Beck area and roped them down. It was a long, interesting night. Pies followed.

The next day I was back at work. The pager went off again. 'Search. Group of two stuck in Langdale.' We found them in the Bright Beck area and roped them down. It was a long, exhausting night. Pies followed.

At the time I was really surprised that people would go out into such conditions without basic gear. But now a missing person's lack of basic equipment doesn't surprise me at all!"

Michael Machell

...2009...

133 callouts

February accidents

"Sadly the otherwise stunning conditions in February caught some people out, resulting in a number of fatalities and serious injuries. Team members turned out again and again to face some epic rescues lasting many hours in dangerous conditions, where one false move would have resulted in our sharing the same fate as the unfortunate people that we were trying to rescue."

Nick Owen Team Leader's Report

"Waiting in the cold at the foot of a treacherous icy fell – waiting anxiously for the lights of the Team as they slowly descend – blinded by many headtorches as a gentle hand on my shoulder signals that the care of the bereaved casualty is being transferred to me in the busy quietness of a long night."

Olena Beal

...2009

133 callouts

November floods

Heavy rain over several days caused houses and businesses to be flooded, sank boats and washed cars away. All roads between Ambleside and elsewhere were impassable. Police, fire, ambulance and county highways were based at Lowfold and local ambulances remained with us for several months until the flooded ambulance station was restored. For several days our new vehicles with air intake snorkels and axle breather pipes were the only way to get around. We rescued people from stranded cars, supported the other emergency services and ferried medical staff around. One of our Land Rovers was damaged when a road collapsed beneath it, but fortunately none of the occupants was injured.

2010 and Beyond

Nick Owen

LAMRT was formed forty years ago "for the public benefit, to relieve suffering and the distress arising among persons and animals endangered by accident, illness or natural hazards in Great Britain and primarily within the area of the Lake District". (LAMRT constitution)

The newly amalgamated Team was a response to a local need. Since that time much has changed and the Team has continued to evolve to meet new challenges. Yet the basic philosophy remains the same and we can still trace our ancestry back to those early ad hoc groups which performed rescues using nothing more advanced than a farmer's gate. To use a quote from Sir Isaac Newton "If I have seen further it is only by standing on the shoulders of giants". Who and what we are now is a direct consequence of the hard work, sacrifice and foresight of our predecessors.

As we move into the next chapter of our history, we are as strong as ever, adapting to meet every new challenge thrown at us. We are still determinedly independent, answerable to no governing body save ourselves, our own fiercest critics. By working this way we can avoid bureaucracy, change quickly to meet demand, but always with our primary objective at the forefront of our minds. We remain slightly anarchic, never turning out in response to any command, but because we think this job is worth doing and we love it with deep passion.

And what greater reward could there be than this: sometimes, just occasionally, we get to save a life.

What's in a location

Nick Owen

People talk about 'conquering' a mountain, but I firmly believe a mountain along with it's weather is a completely benign thing with no supernatural features. However some places do seem to have something about them ...

Three places that have featured regularly in our callouts for forty years are Kirkstone Pass, Crinkle Crags, and Stickle Tarn and the path that climbs to it.

The latter first. Thankfully little by way of tragedy here, but the sheer number of visitors to the Tarn, principally via the main path from New Dungeon Ghyll, means that it is bound to feature in our callout list frequently. Here we see what is probably a microcosm of our rescue effort with an equal balance of leg injuries, other medical problems and the lost/benighted/cragfast. Of course, this path is the main access to Jack's Rake and Pavey Ark, a place probably worthy of its own write up, having been the location of a significant number of fatalities, serious injuries and some very lucky survivors over the years.

Next...Crinkle Crags. There's something about the terrain that leads people astray. It has multiple summits, a tortuous path that weaves its way over the summit ridge more or less north/south. The Bad Step presents its own set of difficulties. A short, moderate scramble, much more difficult to descend than climb, causes many parties to split, some to tackle it, some to go round. In many cases they don't meet again until many hours later in the valley, or at our base! The terrain steers people away from the north-south route, and the (fairly) obvious landmark of Three Tarns, and they usually end up on the steep ground somewhere near the top of Rest Ghyll. A map plotting the location of 'found' people shows many of them in a relatively small area overlooking the ghyll.

Finally, Kirkstone Pass, including Red Screes and the large bowl to its south. It's always been a bit of an iconic place, in keeping with many mountain passes. As a transport link its heyday has passed, but it has left an old coaching inn with a long history. Little of the Teams involvement up there has failed to add to its status. From sledging accidents, via many vehicles stranded in the snow, including a stretch limo, to men with guns avoiding all attempts to find them. It has also been the scene of many serious and fatal incidents, often in winter conditions. In one case we arrived to search for a missing man, to be met by the ethereal sight of a woman in a fur coat, wearing odd shoes, who loomed out of the mist, standing in the middle of the road, clearly very upset. She turned out to be the wife of the missing man. Sadly, he was subsequently located high on the fellside, having died of the injuries sustained in a fall. He was located by Dog Yana; her final 'find' before she retired. A letter written to the Guardian from the family of a local man who died there has moved many people, and still reminds me of the reasons why many of us get involved in mountain rescue. Most of what we do is mundane – sometimes we can save a life, but we always make a difference.

Above Kirkstone

Stickle Ghyll

Crinkle Crags

103

Team Members

joined	name	left	joined	name	left
1970	G Bates	1970		K Drake	1976
	M Waite	1970		C Earnshaw	1992
	C Jones	1970		H Fecitt	1972
	D Wakeford	1970		A Flitters	1998
	B Daly	1970		R Goodson	1990
	B Jones	1970		M Grindrod	1997
	F Davies	1976		R Harding	1974
	S Cross	1976		I Haigh	1980
	P Greenall	1993		S Hulse	2005
	P Bell	1993		D Mounsey	1973
	C Downham	1993		K Ogilvie	1976
	P Allonby	1998		D Oldham	1973
	C Lewis	1976		M Osman	1979
	G Bowen Dr	to present		C Otway	1972
	J Graham	to present		A Roberts	1972
	M Richards	to present		D Robinson	1976
	P Watson	1971			
	E Thompson	1999			
	G Sanders	1976	**1971**	C Atkinson	1976
	C Atkinson	1976		D Earnshaw Dr	1989
	W Barron	1973		A Richards	1999
	R Cambridge	1987		E Penman	1980
	M Cooper	1979		N Wiseman	1872
	E Cross	1972		J Ball	1972
	J Cross	1972		A Bradborn	1972
	R Cook	1970		G Clayton	1972
				C Mortlock	1976

joined	name	left		joined	name	left
1972	A Brammall	1983			J Horne	1980
	C Eatough	1975			J Owen	1977
	S Kelly	1976			J Parker	1982
					I Sadler	1979
1973	J Smith	1975			K Thompkinson	1980
	G Hartley Rev.	to present			I Wall	1982
	T Redfern	1985				
	J Wyatt	1980		**1978**	M Crosby	1979
					M Borrowdale	1983
1974	D Lett	1976				
	M Graham	1979		**1979**	A Cornforth	1982
	D Guest	1979			M Stanning	1982
	C Hall	1976				
	G Harris	1975		**1980**	M Scrowston	1993
	B Morgan	2010			B Yates	1987
	M Penman/Richards	to present			P Monaghan	1987
	J Robinson	1976			B Marshall	1990
	G Spragg	1999			W Hicks	1983
	D Townsend	1976			D Heap	1981
					R Howarth	1982
1975	N Walker	1992			J Gaskell	1992
					I Cockburn Dr	1982
1976	D Wrigglesworth	1980			J Fuller	1994
	P Nattrass	1992				
				1981	C Wright	1997
1977	I Birkett Dr	1987			P Ennis	2005
	M Cornforth	1981				
	P Cornforth	1982		**1982**	T Hodnet	1984
	P Grant	1980			D Owen	1998
					G Russell	1982

joined	name	left		joined	name	left
1983	I Williamson	1990		**1990**	-	
	J White	1993				
	M Withers	2002		**1991**	N Verrall	2005
	J Greenwood	1999			P Seddon	to present
	P Farrand	1998			N Owen	to present
					B Conlon	1994
1984	D Till	to present			M Eccles	2001
	P McDonald	1987			D Almond	to present
	B Laycock	1992				
				1992	P Green	2010
1985	N McVeigh	1999			B Porter	1997
	J Grindrod	to present			S Hollis	1992
	S Fahey	1992			A Nelhams	1999
	M Cocker	1987			D Hodgson	1997
1986	A Boston	to present				
	K Morgan	2006		**1993**	N Fayers	to present
1987	-				A Cooper	to present
					C Anderson	2000
1988	A Tree	1989			M Devereux	1997
	D Thompson	1990			M Capewell	2004
	D Pearson	1988				
	K Miller	to present		**1994**	R Pickup	to present
	M Prince	1999				
	S Milanec	1999		**1995**	P Davies Dr	to present
	A Loudon	1990			J Belshaw	2000
	A Carling	1994			R Wilson	2005
	J E Smith	2005				
				1996	P Noble	2004
1989	J Clark	1992			C Kehoe Dr	1999

joined	name	left		joined	name	left
	K Hopwood	2003		**2003**	P Burke	to present
	A Hill	1999			M Mitchell	2007
	J Archer	2003		**2004**	L Noble	to present
	J Stanley Dr	2003			D Davies	to present
					K Birch	to present
1997	K Grindrod	to present				
	A Finlayson	2007		**2005**	-	
	M Fearon	to present				
				2006	O Beal	to present
1998	-				O Benson	to present
1999	M Kenyon	2007		**2007**	A Kaufman	2007
	G Sisson	2005			M Bains	to present
	S Horner	2000			R Brookes	to present
2000	D Barrington	to present		**2008**	MDalek	to present
	D Gallagher	2001			S Pendered	to present
	C Judge	2007			J Dyson	to present
	B Petty	2003				
	J Sayer	to present		**2009**	S McDearmid	to present
	D Visser	2003			N Kirkham	to present
					M Lynchey	to present
2001	S Mackenzie	to present			M Machell	to present
	P Taylor	to present			G Lobb	to present
	S Halton	2008			G Barrington	to present
					L Mallabon	to present
2002	P Barnes	2009				
	S White	2007				

Search Dogs

Year Graded	Dog	Breed	Handler
1973	Jan	Irish Setter	Malcolm Grindrod
1974	Claiff	German Shepherd	John Wyatt
1976	Sally	Irish Setter	Malcolm Grindrod
1976	Tasha	Border Collie / Cross	Andrew Bramall
1976	Celt	German Shepherd	Tom Redfern
1978	Banner	German Shepherd	Roy Harding
1978	Spot	Border Collie	Malcolm Grindrod
1979	Spin	Border Collie	Malcolm Grindrod
1980	Vicky	Lab / Collie	Peter Nattrass
1982	Bess	Labrador	Jim Fuller
1982	Dart	German Shepherd	John Gaskell
1984	Tag	Bordor Collio	Jim Groonwood
1984	Jan	Border Collie	Malcolm Grindrod
1986	Mist	Border Collie	Malcolm Grindrod
1985	Loch	Border Collie	David Riley
1990	Anna	Border Collie	Joy Grindrod
1998	Paddy	Border Collie	Roger Pickup
1999	Yana	Border Collie	Nick Fayers
2003	Sky	Border Collie	Christine Judge
2008	Beinn	Border Collie	Roger Pickup
2009	Kitt	Border Collie	Olly Benson

Dogs training in 2009 and expected to grade 2010:

	Dog	Breed	Handler
	Einich	Border Collie	Joy Grindrod
	Sam	Border Collie	Nick Fayers

A Chronology

1970	The two teams amalgamated
	Sid Cross became Team Leader
	Land Rover kept at Wateredge until space was offered in Lowfold barn
1971	A second Land Rover bought
1972	Peter Bell given £100 to develop a new split stretcher
	Lowfold bought and internal improvements begun
1973	Peter Greenall became Team Leader
	Two new Land Rovers bought
	Entonox used for the first time
	Improvements to Lowfold completed
	First search dog graded
1974	First helicopter training
	First helicopter rescue
1975	Bell Stretchers now widely used
	Reviva used for first time
	Blackpool Tower abseil
1976	Eric (Spider) Penman became Team Leader
	First landline connected radio
1977	House bell callout system
1979	First time Sea King helicopter used
1980	Bedford ambulance bought
1981	Space created to garage three vehicles at Lowfold
1982	Tom Redfern became Team Leader
	Tone only pagers used for first time
	Rocket launcher bought
1984	Team Land Rover caught fire
1985	Stewart Hulse became Team Leader
	Two new Land Rovers bought
	Extendable radio mast bought
	First medical seminar
1987	First defibrillator bought
1988	Advanced casualty care group began IV access training
	Lockerbie Disaster
1989	VW Synchro ambulance bought
1993	Ada's Nook completed
	First time radios supplied to all team members
	Portable fax machine bought to use on the fell
1995	First message pagers
	First GPS units acquired

1996	New Land Rover ambulance	2002	National Lottery Grant awarded
	First encounter with a personal locator beacon		Lowfold demolished in November
	Urban myth began		Ambleside coach crash
1997	Ice rescue sledge bought	2003	New base completed
	GPS bought for night searches	2004	Morecambe Bay Cocklers Disaster
	First prototype GPS team member tracking system		Changed to High Band radios
			Helicopter crash in Mickleden
1998	First LAMRT website	2006	Nick Owen became Team Leader
	Sid Cross died		MRMap GPS tracking system
1999	Fundraising started for new base		Two satellite phones bought
2000	Mark Eccles became Team Leader	2007	Grayrigg train derailment
	New base planned and planning permission obtained		Swiftwater rescue training started
	LAMRT became limited company	2008	Two new Land Rover first response vehicles bought
2001	Nick Verrall became Team Leader	2009	New Land Rover people carrier and new ambulance bought
	First time assisted by air ambulance		
	Stewart Hulse awarded MBE		Warning signs placed in Langdale due to winter conditions
	Fells closed due to Foot and Mouth Disease		Severe flooding in November
	Adjacent property bought to enable base redevelopment		First training website
	Medical telemetry transmitted from fell in TETRA trial		First Plain English Guide to Drugs in Mountain Rescue